MIDLAND RED BUSES

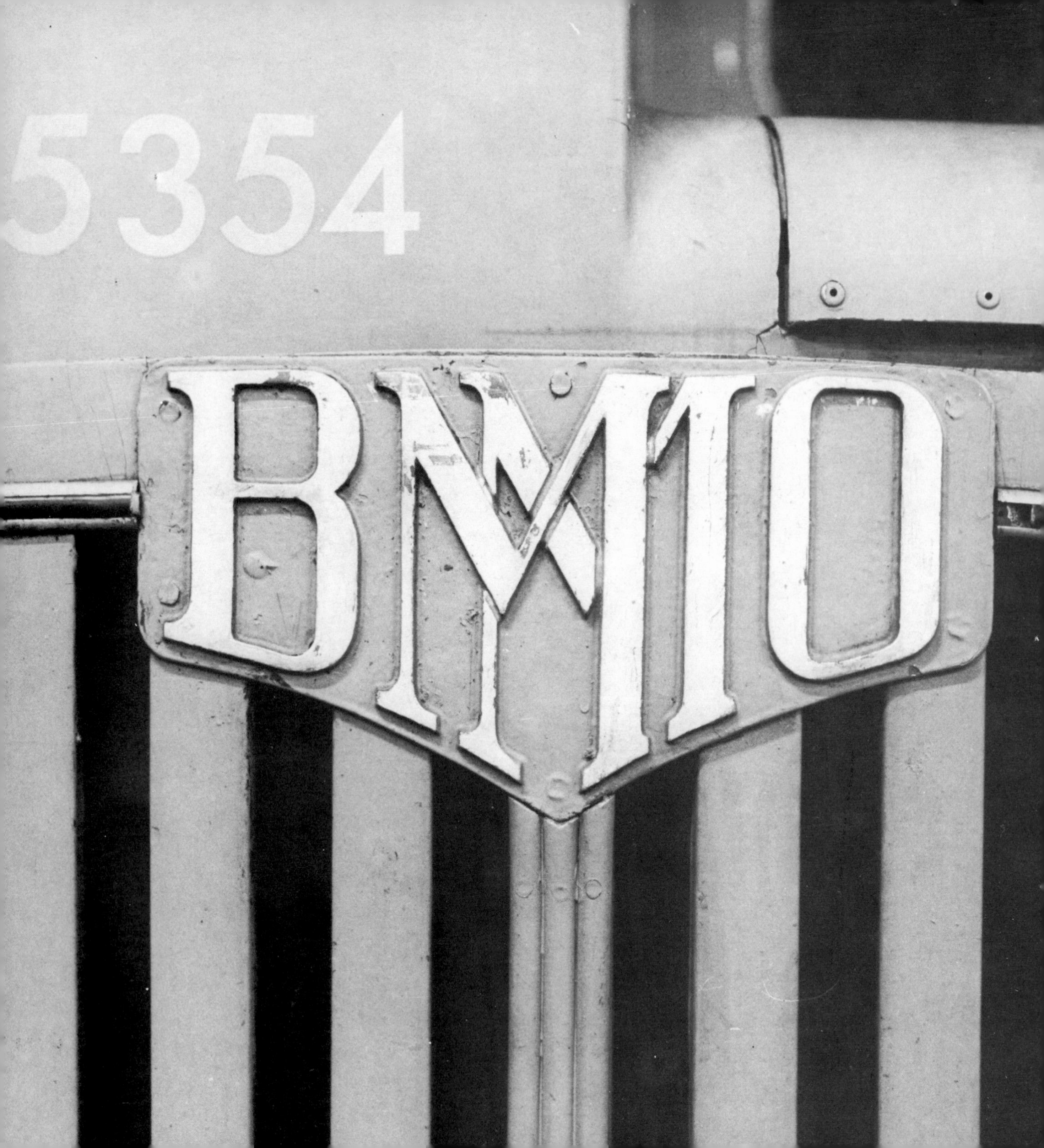
5354
BMO

MIDLAND RED BUSES

M.W. GREENWOOD

D. BRADFORD BARTON LIMITED

INTRODUCTION

This album comes as a tribute to the buses and coaches manufactured by the Birmingham and Midland Motor Omnibus Company, at a time when the remaining examples are reaching the Autumn and, in some cases, the Winter of their life, and to the many people who designed and developed this exclusive breed.

Midland Red, as the company was to become better known, commenced production of its own vehicles in 1923 and it was these, and their successors, which made the company unique for almost fifty years. The story really started in late 1904, when Midland Red was founded to operate motorbuses on behalf of the British Electric Traction Company in the Black Country. Operations eventually commenced in mid-1905 with a small but assorted collection of double-deck vehicles inherited from the defunct Birmingham Motor Express Company Limited. This original fleet was unreliable and soon sold off, being replaced by horse buses!

The horse buses, however, were not competitive with the new electric tramcars being used in the area and motorbuses were reintroduced in 1912. At the same time L.G.Wyndham Shire was appointed Chief Engineer. A gifted engineer, he constantly introduced improvements to the large number of Tilling-Stevens on which the fleet had become standardised. In the early 1920s, Mr.Shire proposed that it would be in the company's best interest to produce its own vehicles. The proposal was accepted and so an era commenced.

The chassis produced by Midland Red were designated S.O.S., the first eventually being christened 'Standard'. The true meaning of the initials S.O.S. is not known. This was a well-kept secret, but evidence has been established which suggests both 'Shire's Omnibus Specification' and 'Superior Omnibus Specification'. However, it has not been possible to totally verify either version. The S.O.Ss were highly advanced machines and during the 1930s and 1940s, apart from its own large intake, vehicles were also supplied to other British Electric Traction associated fleets.

The S.O.S. remained in production until 1940 when the final S.O.S. - a S.O.N. saloon - was completed.

When Mr.Shire retired in the Spring of 1940, Midland Red operations had expanded to cover most of the Midland counties and services were run almost entirely by Midland Red-manufactured vehicles. Donald Sinclair succeeded as Chief Engineer, and in 1943 he became the company's first General Manager. Prior to this, there had never been a General Manager, the company being very successfully run by O.C.Power as Traffic Manager and Mr.Shire in his engineering capacity. Following his retirement, the S.O.S. designation was superseded by the well known B.M.M.O. marque.

Mr.Sinclair, who served with the company for over 26 years before retiring, will probably be best remembered for his pioneering development of the underfloor-engined single-deck bus which put the company many years ahead of outside chassis manufacturers - an enviable achievement for such a relatively small producer. Under his guidance two underfloor-engined double-deckers were built in 1960-1 but, regrettably, the type never went into production.

As the need to replace the old fleet outpaced the production of new vehicles, outside manufacturers supplied conventional models in increasing numbers. Following Nationalisation, which Midland Red opposed, and incorporation into the National Bus Company in 1968, the fate of the manufacturing interests of Midland Red was sealed. The final B.M.M.O. S.23 single-deck chassis was completed in 1970, the last of a long line of individual, advanced and remarkably successful vehicles.

Midland Red-built vehicles did not often find further service with other operators after withdrawal, which is the main reason why only a handful of pre-war models have been secured by preservationists. The leading preservation society is the Birmingham and Midland Motor Omnibus Trust, who have in their care a unique collection of former Midland Red vehicles covering the period from 1925 to 1965. In addition, they are currently working on an ambitious Midland Bus Museum project at Wythall, near Bromsgrove. I would strongly urge anyone who is interested or concerned about Midland Red vehicles to contact the Trust's secretary, J.A.Seale, at 61 Stornoway Road, Castle Vale, Birmingham.

This album is intended to portray photographically the development of the S.O.S. and B.M.M.O. marques rather than a history of the company. Whilst I hope I have achieved a reasonable coverage of vehicles, in some cases

important models have not been represented because no quality photographs exist - or any that do have been widely published before.

Finally, I would like to express my thanks to the contributing photographers and especially to Paul Gray of Birmingham and Midland Motor Omnibus Trust for all his help and advice.

The 'Standard' S.O.S. of 1923 was the first model produced by the Midland Red company. It was literally a revolution in British bus design with pneumatic tyres, high seating capacity, lightweight construction and exceptional reliability. The majority of the early models were based on the Tilling-Stevens T.S.3 but fitted with a more reliable gearbox and plate clutch transmission. Early chassis frames were actually built by Tillings, including Brush-bodied 334 (HA 2334).   B.M.M.O.

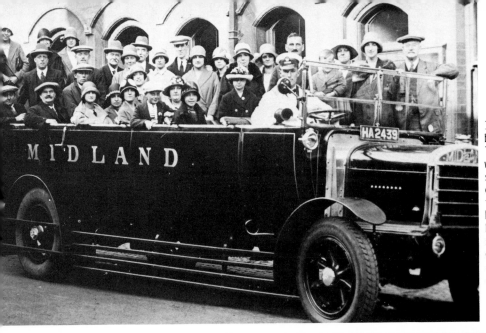

In addition to the bus-bodied 'Standards', a large number of char-a-bancs were also placed into service with a seating capacity of 32, the same as the bus version, all the bodies being built by Davidson. 439 (HA 2439) is seen with a full complement of passengers. Note that apart from one gentleman and one young boy, everyone is wearing some sort of headgear!
   B.A.M.M.O.T. Collection

Fifty-one 'Standard'
S.O.Ss were rebodied
with United 26-seat
bodies in 1929, being
later upseated to
thirty. These were
classed S.O.S. O.D.
and 407 (HA 2407) is
seen on 6 May 1935
at Bearwood,
Birmingham, complete
with flags for the
Silver Jubilee of
King George V. She
lasted in this form
until 1938.

B.M.M.O.

MIDLAND RED

ROMSLEY
VIA QUINTON & HALESOWEN

The F.S. was a logical development of the 'Standard' S.O.S. Constructed in 1926, they were of a forward control layout allowing increased body space, and consequently an increase of two in the seating capacity. Eighteen received 34-seat char-a-banc bodies by Davidson, including 528 (HA 3528). They were to last only three years in this form, being drastically rebuilt to single-deckers using converted double-deck bodies from early Tilling-Stevens chassis. The classification F.S. is believed to have stood for 'Forward Steering', although 'Future Standard' has also been recorded as being the correct meaning. Again, it is not known which is correct. Following conversion the char-a-bancs were classified O.D. ('Old Deckers').

B.M.M.O.

9

The S.O.S. M ('Madam') first made its appearance in 1929, using Q.L. type chassis but with improved bodies featuring more comfortable seats, the concept being designed to attract women passengers to do their shopping, etc. - by bus! With the increase in comfort came a decrease in capacity from 37 to 34. The first prototype featured the straight sides and rocker panels of the Q.L., but the other prototype and all the production models received gently curved sides. Three Ransomes-bodied examples, 918 (HA 4918), 910 (HA 4910) and 929 (HA 4929) are portrayed above, complete with white wartime markings and headlamp masks.

1927 Midland Red produced the S.O.S. Q ('Queen'). This model was developed to obtain the maximum capacity within the same overall dimensions of the F.S. type. This was achieved by moving the bulkhead forward as far as possible, increasing the seating capacity to 37. In order to allow the driver more room the engine, bonnet and radiator were moved off-centre towards the near side. This became a feature on all subsequent S.O.S. half-cabs. All the were withdrawn by the end of 1936, with the example illustrated being used as a shed, a common fate of pre-war Midland Red saloons following withdrawal.   A.G.Willis

sically similar to the Q was the S.O.S. Q.L. ('Queen Low') of 1928. The chief improvements re four-wheeled brakes and a reduction in height brought about by using smaller disc wheels. e that had a particularly long life was 781 (HA 3781), with 37-seat Brush body. She ceived a complete overhaul and repaint following arduous war service at Rugby and wasn't nally withdrawn until 1950. She is pictured late in life carrying post-war fleet number 862.
                                                                                S.E.Letts

Starting life in 1930, 163 (HA 6163) was an S.O.S. C.O.D. ('Clarke's Omnibus Design').
Mr.Clarke was the Chief Engineer of the Trent Motor Traction Company and the nominal
designer of the original model. Not surprisingly, Trent took delivery of a large
proportion of this type. Following the fitting of a new Short Brothers body, 163 was
reclassified S.O.S. I.M. ('Improved Madam') in 1931. The original Brush body went to a
new S.O.S. I.M.6 ('Improved Madam 6') chassis. After the commencement of production of
the I.M.6 Class, the entire I.M. Class became known as I.M.4s. On training duties,
HA 6163 is seen at Bearwood, Birmingham, c.1949. By this time she had received her
post-war fleet number, 1158. Close behind are Q.L. HA 4838, by then a 21-year-old
youngster, and at the rear F.E.D.D. double-decker FHA 822.   G.H.Stone

Many S.O.Ss were supplied to associated British Electric Traction fleets, of which CN 5478, an S.O.S. I.M.6, was a fine representative. Note the cast 'Northern' plate on the radiator. The I.M.6 was very similar visually to the I.M.4 but was powered by the six-cylinder, 5.986 litre S.O.S. RR25B engine. The B.E.T. supply arrangement lasted until 1940 when the final S.O.S.-manufactured vehicles, a batch of fourteen S.O.Ns, were delivered to the Trent company.

B.M.M.O.

A number of S.O.S. I.M.6s were converted to producer gas operation during the war years. About thirty buses were so equipped, and these were allocated to predetermined routes operated by only a few garages: Banbury, Bearwood, Digbeth, Hereford, Hinckley, Rugby and Tamworth, with Evesham garage being totally equipped with a gas fleet (nine buses). There was considerable interchange of vehicles between these garages, especially when common routes were involved. A good detailed close-up of a standard trailer, as towed by a 1933 I.M.6 (HA 8317), can be seen. Note the white wartime markings on both the bus and trailer and the 'leopard spot' garage code immediately above the bus's registration plate. This particular 'leopard spot' indicates Birmingham (Digbeth) as the present user.

B.M.M.O.

From magnificent beast to derelict veteran. An imposing contrast between Short-bodied I.M.6 HA 8318, photographed towards the end of her life, and Brush-bodied I.M.4 HA 8251 as a contractor's site bus, complete with chimney!

A.B.Cross

With the withdrawal of the open-top Tilling-Stevens double-deck vehicle in 1929 the entire Midland Red fleet became single-deck. This situation had to change with the growth of services in the industrial Black Country, and for this reason a prototype rear entrance double-decker was built in 1931, with fifty production versions entering service in 1932-3. Bodywork was shared between four builders, Short, Brush, Eastern Counties and Metro-Cammell, and were classified S.O.S. D.D.-R.E. ('Double-Decker - Rear Entrance'). By 1940 the entire class was centred on Leicester, with HA 8001/3-12 at Coalville, HA 8013-36 at Southgate Street and HA 8037-50 at Sandacre Street. HA 8002 never entered service with Midland Red, being sold to Northern General Transport when new. At rest in Leicester, HA 8036 with Brush bodywork was photographed on 16 July 1939.

J.E.Cull

The S.O.S. O.N. ('Onward') was introduced in 1934 to take advantage of the then maximum length of 27' 6" for two-axle single-deckers. This increased length and compact engine allowed a capacity for 38 passengers. Three O.Ns were fitted with experimental indirect injection diesel engines and classified D.O.N. ('Diesel Onward'). A production batch of D.O.Ns followed, although owing to the fitting of a larger size diesel engine six inches were lost in the main body section, reducing the capacity to 36. O.N. bodies were built by Short Brothers with D.O.N. bodies being built by both Short and Brush. In 1935 B.M.M.O. evolved its own diesel engine which did not affect bonnet length, and were subsequently fitted into 44 O.Ns. The vehicles involved were classified C.O.N. ('Converted O.N.'). Leicester-based O.N. AHA 512 retained its original petrol engine until withdrawal in 1952. Note the wooden chock placed under the back wheel to prevent the vehicle from rolling.

R.Marshall

Pictured in the sn⟨ ⟩
of the 1947 winter ⟨ ⟩
Keresley near Cove⟨ ⟩
a 1934 Short Broth⟨ ⟩
bodied O.N., 1596 ⟨ ⟩
(AHA 491), awaits
attention in the p⟨ ⟩
wintry sunshine af⟨ ⟩
being out in the c⟨ ⟩
all night. Note t⟨ ⟩
it was still fitte⟨ ⟩
with wartime
headlights.
  T.W.Moore Collect⟨ ⟩

Following the introduction of the S.O.S. D.D.-R.E., and with all its single-deckers being of a forward entrance layout, the company took the logical step and decided to produce a modern front entrance double-decker. A prototype was constructed in 1933 and its styling was very much along the lines of the rear entrance double-deckers. A production batch of 56-seat Short Brothers-bodied vehicles were delivered in 1934. These original fifty vehicles were followed by a further 135 Metro-Cammell-bodied machines in 1935-6 and 150 Brush-bodied examples in 1938-9. The class was originally designated D.D.-F.E., but by 1936 had become identified by the more familiar title F.E.D.D. ('Front Entrance Double-Decker'). BHA 820 was a 1936 Metro-Cammell-bodied example.

Brush-bodied FHA 210 was delivered in 1938. Originally fitted with half-drop windows, extensive reconstruction of the Brush-bodied vehicles took place in the early post-war period. The work was carried out on FHA 210 by Aero and Engineering (Merseyside) Ltd., Hooton, the most noticeable change being the new rubber-mounted windows with sliding ventilators. The introduction of spray painting led to unrelieved red in contrast to BHA 820. The F.E.D.D. Class was the last S.O.S. double-decker to be produced.

T.W.Moore

In October 1942 Brush-bodied F.E.D.D. EHA 299 was rebuilt with what became the 'new look' front, featuring a full-width bonnet and a concealed radiator and which set the trend for post-war production. It reverted to exposed radiator layout upon rebuilding of the bodywork in 1951, but it retained non-standard upper deck front windows, eventually being withdrawn in 1960.

B.M.M.O.

A 'normal' example from the first batch of Brush-bodied F.E.D.Ds was EHA 273. Tradition was broken on this batch, as the fuel tank was moved from its usual position (for S.O.Ss) under the driver's seat to the off side front of the chassis frame. On the subsequent batches of Brush-bodied F.E.D.Ds the fuel tank reverted to beneath the driver's seat. It was observed in Pool Meadow, Coventry, on a cold wintry day in 1954 about to make its way to its home town. Extensively reconstructed, it was to last for a further four years in service. A post-war D.7 and two post-war single-deckers complete the picture.   D.Morris

A view of Stourbridge garage and bus station in the mid-1930s offers a good selection of contemporary S.O.S. marques. Five Metro-Cammell-bodied F.E.D.Ds intermingle with a pair of 1935 Short Brothers-bodied D.O.Ns and a 1931 I.M.4. The garage, which was opened in 1926, comprised full garaging facilities and a large forecourt which acted as a bus station. Also provided on this impressive corner site were offices, workshops and an enquiry office. The garage itself was of steel framed two-bay construction, but differed from similar Midland Red structures of that time in that the exterior walls were metal sheeting instead of brick. Three entrance/exits on the frontage led on to the bus station. The property was slightly extended in 1931 and, from that time, could accommodate 47 vehicles.

Fifty new coaches were built in 1937 and classified S.L.R. ('Saloon Low Rolls-Royce'). They were built to a forward-control configuration and fitted with 30-seat English Electric bodies. The bodies featured a sliding entrance door and a full-width cab with concealed radiator, a feature well ahead of its time. A Coronation year view of CHA 891 awaiting trippers to Llandudno, Rhyl and Colwyn Bay portrays the pleasing appearance of these vehicles. In 1948 it had been converted from its original petrol engine to a Leyland diesel engine, as well as receiving a new grille and simplified mouldings. D.Morris

The entire class of S.L.Rs was withdrawn in 1955. Two were retained for non-P.S.V. use by Midland Red whilst the rest were sold to a London dealer. Most found further users, including a number that ended their working careers in the sunnier climes of the Canary Islands and Cyprus! CHA 990, shortly before withdrawal, appears to have seen plenty of action, judging from the condition of the front mudguards! A.B.Cross

CHA 962 was one of the two S.L.Rs retained by Midland Red as dual control training vehicles. Based at Bearwood, Birmingham, it is seen at that garage in July 1961, by which time it had been repainted into an unrelieved all-over red livery.   P.Kingston

In 1935 a prototype of a new class of saloon bus, designated S.O.N. ('Saloon Onward'), was constructed. Fitted with a Short Brothers 38-seat body, it was powered by the standard S.O.S. RR2SB petrol engine. The production models delivered from 1936 to 1940 were, however, fitted with the 8 litre K type oil engines, so the prototype was reclassified O.N. The batches up to 1938 were fitted with English Electric bodywork, whilst the vehicles built in 1939 and 1940 received Brush bodywork. EHA 741 formed part of the third batch of English Electric-bodied vehicles delivered in 1938. Unlike the first batch of S.O.Ns the 1937 and 1938 models were never heavily rebuilt in later life. Following experiments on a small variety of S.O.Ss electric saloon heating was specified for the 1938 S.O.Ns and all subsequent S.O.S. single-deckers. Note the unusual position of the near side wing mirror.

The 1939 FHA series S.O.Ns were similar in appearance to the previous batch but the bodies were built by Brush. They were the first single-deckers with the new style radiator. A 1958 view finds 2331 (FHA 486) awaiting a driver at Coventry. The bodies on this batch were rebuilt between 1949 and 1951 by Hooton and Nudd Brothers & Lockyer, resulting in the loss of waist rail mouldings and full drop windows.

The last S.O.Ss built for the company's use were fifty Brush-bodied S.O.Ns
delivered in 1940. These particular bodies were of a more rounded design producing
rather attractive vehicles. A new improved type of seating was fitted and, for the
first time, used ticket boxes were provided. Again the majority were rebuilt in
the early post-war period, including 2403 (GHA 322), ready for the return of the
football crowds at Villa Park in 1951.
D.Morris

An example from the first batch of S.O.Ns was rebuilt to full front and dual control layout for driver training purposes in 1952. Until withdrawn from its ancillary capacity in 1962, CHA 551 was based at Bearwood garage.
D.Morris

S.O.Ss did not often find further service with other operators after withdrawal. However, a regular demand for redundant S.O.Ss came from showmen. That became the fate of 1939 S.O.N. FHA 469 following withdrawal in 1957.
G.H.Stone

English Electric-bodied S.O.N. DHA 731 of 1937 was converted into a tree-cutter in 1955 for the associated fleet of Stratford-upon-Avon Blue Motors, who numbered it T.C.1. It was withdrawn in 1964 and ended its useful life in a Warwickshire scrapyard, dumped and forgotten.

T.W.Moore

The last fourteen S.O.S. chassis which immediately
followed the GHA series for B.M.M.O. were supplied to
Trent, an associated B.E.T. (British Electric Traction)
fleet. Trent recently repurchased one of its former 1939
Willowbrook-bodied S.O.Ns in a very dilapidated state,
from a showman, and completely rebuilt it. The photographs
show RC 7927 at Trent's Derby depot open day on
30 September 1979 following complete restoration, and
the state of the vehicle at Dalby Wolds, Leicestershire,
on Christmas Eve 1977. Note the T.M.T. (Trent Motor
Traction) emblem in the middle of the radiator in lieu of
Midland Red's S.O.S. or later B.M.M.O. emblems.

M.W.Greenwood

30

The first new S.O.S. coaches with diesel engines were the
O.N.C. Class ('Onward Coach'). Built in 1939, they
totalled 25 in number and were fitted with Duple 30-seat
coachwork. Similar in general appearance to the earlier
S.L.R. Class, they were plainer and avoided being
over-elaborate. The sliding roof on the O.N.C. Class
made them ideal for special occasions and for this reason
one member of the class, 2286 (FHA 218), enjoyed an
extended life. On 26 May 1963 it had the task of
carrying members of the Leicester City Football Club to
the Town Hall, Leicester, to meet local dignitaries
following their appearance in the F.A. Cup Final.

O.N.C. 2272 (FHA 4
in final form,
captured on a day
trip to Aberystwyt
in July 1960.
Withdrawal came la
in the year, by wh
time the coach was
over twenty years
old! A remarkable
tribute to the
mechanical designe
and coach builders
these fine machine
                P.Kings

Having lost its ty
FHA 416 was lookin
somewhat sorry for
itself when
photographed at
Hixon near Staffor
in late 1963.
                A.G.Wil

One hundred single-deckers delivered in 1946-7 represented the fruition of wartime development work. They started a new fleet number series commencing at 3000 and were classified S.6. The body design evolved from a number of wartime prototypes (classified S.1-S.5) and was built in equal numbers by Brush and Metro-Cammell. The illuminated 'Midland' sign fitted below the windscreen was to feature on all Midland Red vehicles up to and including the S.19 type. All the early post-war single-deckers were later lengthened to take advantage of revised maximum length dimensions. Fortunately the long wheelbase with the rear axle placed well back suited the conversion work which was carried out by Roe of Leeds in 1953, increasing the capacity by four seats to a total of 44.

B.M.M.O.

A rear destination roller blind was fitted to the S.6 and was adopted as standard for the post-war single- and double-deck fleet until the mid-1960s. Later this was reduced to just a three-track number blind. The emergency door was in its traditional Midland Red position at the centre of the rear end. The small wooden block on the lower off side of the rear was for garage identification code commonly known as the 'leopard spots'. With its underfloor engine and front entrance, the S.6 was immensely important as the trendsetter for single-deckers throughout the country. It took other manufacturers between four and five years before they could market anything that matched the advance design of the S.6.   B.M.M.O.

By July 1961 3024's Metro-Cammell body had been lengthened by Roe. It stands next to Brush-bodied 3080 (HHA 681) in Worcester bus station.　　A.G.Willis

Midland Red-built buses rarely saw further service with other operators due to the problems with spares. However, undeterred, Hulley's of Baslow, Derbyshire purchased former Brush-bodied S.6 3096 along with an S.8 and two S.9s in the early 1960s. Resplendent 3096 is seen in Hulley's red and grey livery.　　P.Gray

The first post-war Midland Red coaches were based on the single-deck service bus S.6. The C.1 Class delivered in 1948 and 1949 were fitted with 30-seat Duple bodywork incorporating a central sliding entrance door. Twelve very similar C.2 Class coaches followed in 1950, intended primarily for extended tours and thus having a seating capacity for only 26. C.2 3349 (KHA 349) shows off its outward-opening passenger door, another variation from the C.1 Class, to good effect whilst unloading at Coventry on 26 August 1961.

P.Kingston

C.1s 3307 and 3340 pose together during a rest period on a day tour. These coaches withstood the passage of time and lasted well into the 1960s. Both of these vehicles were retained by the company following withdrawal for use on driver training duties. The majority of C.1s retained for training were converted to dual control, including 3308 (KHA 308). Working from Nuneaton garage, it was leaving Coventry when photographed, being pursued by rear-engined Coventry Corporation vehicles, in the Summer of 1970.

A small number of touring coaches were still required in the early 1960s, and although four C.2s were modernised they were still getting on in years for coach cruise work. Therefore, three (3346, 3350, 3352) were rigorously overhauled in 1962 and rebodied with 26-seat front entrance Plaxton Embassy bodies, being redesignated C.L.2. The C.L.2 machines were used on a variety of duties including occasional stage carriage work; however, 3350 heads through Stafford with a private party in the Summer of 1965.   A.G.Willis

One hundred S.9 type vehicles were built in 1949, and these received bodies constructed by Brush at Loughborough. The single line rear destination box was replaced by a single large three-track number box midway through the S.9 series, and this practice was maintained for many years. Sitting patiently in the High Street, Evesham, 3359 (LHA 359) has completed a journey on local service E13.

A.G.Willis

and Red took full advantage of the new permitted wider dimension of 8' 0" on its next ch of single-deckers. Appropriately classified S.8 (the S.7 code was never used), one red models were built in 1948-9, all with 40-seat Metro-Cammell bodywork. These, like S.6, were lengthened and reseated by Roe from 1951 to 1953. On 3 October 1964 (JHA 894) edges its way out of the Old Warwick Road garage at Leamington under the hful eye of Mickey French (in the white coat), Leamington's Engineering Superintendent.

ntrast in rear ends is offered by this November 1963 Sunday morning view of (from to right) S.13 3935, S.8 3210 and S.14 4287 on the Rugby garage forecourt.

P.Kingston

A number of S.9s were
purchased by Fletcher, the
building contractor, in
1963 in order to provide
staff transport. Former
3376 (LHA 376) stands at
Tittensor, situated
between Stafford and
Stoke-on-Trent, in
May 1964.   A.G.Willis

One of the two S.9s (former
3400) purchased by Hulley's
passes through the
picturesque village of
Baslow, Derbyshire on its
way to Bakewell, having
arrived on the main route
from Chesterfield.

                    P.Gray

Delivery of the S.10 Class began in 1949, 145 vehicles being eventually constructed, and they received bodywork by both Brush and Metro-Cammell. Two further vehicles in the same number series but with detail differences were completed. The prototype S.13 was 3694 and 3703 was a solitary S.11, being basically an S.10 with modified suspension. Brush-bodied S.10 3611 (NHA 611) is given the 'all clear' from the semaphore signal to cross the single-track spur line close to Shrub Hill station, Worcester.   P.Kingston

One of the final S.12s, 3771 (NHA 771), unloads in The Parade, Leamington Spa, having just arrived from Coventry during March 1966. It was to be withdrawn later in the year.

T.W.Moore

1950 revised vehicle dimensions allowed a maximum length of 30' 0" for single-deckers. ...dland Red's S.12 Class was built in 1950-1 to a length of 29' 3", permitting 44 seats ...be fitted. Bodywork once more was shared between Metro-Cammell and Brush. Fitted ...th a Metro-Cammell body, S.12 3738 (NHA 738) lasted until 1966. On 18 August 1965 it ...s working Shrewsbury local service S2 to Berwick Avenue.

A.G.Willis

...ush-bodied S.10 3712 lies idle in Worcester bus station late in its life. The S.10s ...came the final class to have their bodies extended by Roe.

A.G.Willis

The production version of the B.M.M.O. post-war double-decker appeared in 1949 and was an 8' 0" wide version of the D.1 prototype that had been evolved during the war years. One hundred vehicles were delivered in 1949-50 with open platform rear entrances. Bodywork was by Brush with seating capacity for 56. Designated D.5 (the A.D.2 was a post-war A.E.C.-built double-decker and the codes D.3-D.4 were never used), they were always highly commended for their quietness and smooth running qualities - thought by some to have been unequalled in the U.K. post-war bus industry. In the Autumn of their lives 3530 (MHA 530), a Stafford-based machine, stands with S.6 3084 (HHA 685).

A.G.Willis

In 1950 delivery of a further one hundred Brush-bodied double-deckers commenced. Known as the D.5B, they were fitted with electrically-operated four-leaf folding entrance doors. These buses led to the trend for platform doors which are now universally accepted. At Coventry in 1955, D.5B 3795 (NHA 795) waits on stand three ready to continue its journey to Leicester, whilst its conductress struggles in search of a light! This bus was sold to a Midland racetrack owner after withdrawal in 1964 to act as a static scoreboard and control vehicles, and thus had its engine and the majority of its running units removed. It was fortunately rescued for preservation by the Birmingham and Midland Motor Omnibus Trust (B.A.M.M.O.T.) in 1978, who will need to complete a great deal of restoration work before it appears in anything like original condition.   D.Morris

A splendid early 1960s photograph of Dudley bus station, with the castle in the distance, depicts D.5Bs 3799 (NHA 799) and 3862 (NHA 862) on Dudley local service, whilst D.7 4129 (THA 129) clambers up the hill on its way to Cradley Heath, having arrived from Wednesbury.   T.W.Moore

The S.13 production models
entered service between
1951 and 1953, the prototype
3694 having been built in
1950. The first two models
were constructed as buses,
with the remainder being
built to a dual purpose
configuration. The bodies
were manufactured by either
Brush or Nudd Brothers
& Lockyer, and included
two-piece folding doors at
the entrance. During 1956
the 96 dual purpose
40-seaters were repainted
into the then current coach
livery of red with a black
roof, greatly improving the
appearance of these models.
Brush-bodied 3935 (OHA 935)
is seen in this form at
Coventry in 1958.

T.W.Moore

ting for custom, D.5B 3837 sits in Hinckley bus station on local service H21 to Wolvery
d, Burbage. 3837 characterises the somewhat sad expression being emitted from the
iator grille of this class and the early post-war single-deck vehicles. The D.5s/D.5Bs
e withdrawn over the period 1962 to 1967, 3837 lasting until October 1966.

Another Brush-bodied S.13, 3945 (OHA 945), approaches Banbury Cross from Coventry in May 1964.
Withdrawal of the class commenced in that year, with the final vehicle lasting until 1967.

The first B.M.M.O. double-decker built to a lightweight standard was the D.7 Class (the code G.D.6 had been used for a number of Guy double-deck buses). Produced over the period 1953 to 1957, 350 models were completed, all of which received Metro-Cammell bodies based on the builders' newly introduced Orion design. During May 1963, 4424 (VHA 424) was found in Chipping Camden, waiting to make its return journey on the 525 service to Stratford-upon-Avon. Allocated to Bromsgrove, it was somewhat unusual to find it operating on this service. It had a long career at Bromsgrove, being withdrawn from that garage in May 1971.　　　A.G.Willis

ading at Lichfield bus station on 13 May 1961, 3939 (OHA 939) has completed about half of
distance on the long Birmingham to Derby express service.

-bodied S.13 3958 (OHA 958) leaves Pershore on its way to Worcester in May 1963. The
-bodied vehicles had slightly cleaner lines, especially around the front. By this time
had received an S.14 style radiator grille and coach seats from redundant C.3 bodies.
　　　　　　A.G.Willis

7 from the first batch,
(THA 124), basks in the
1960s Summer sunshine in
ford. Originally a
eater, it was upseated
3 in 1955. A.G.Willis

mington-based D.7 4531
A 531) in its home town
1 March 1966. Withdrawn
March 1972 it was
verted, along with
even other D.7s, into a
ing lorry. Much modified,
lost its upper deck,
irs and rear platform,
entered service in its
guise during July 1972
Digbeth garage,
mingham. It passed to
t Midlands P.T.E. in
3, when most B.M.M.O.
vices and vehicles in the
t Midlands metropolitan
nty area passed to that
erator. T.W.Moore

o D.7s to find further
rvice with another
erator were former 4082
HA 82) and 4759 (759 BHA).
rchased by Green's of
ierley Hill 4082, from the
rst batch, entered service
th them in December 1971,
ving spent four years as a
aining vehicle with
dland Red; 4759, from the
st batch, was purchased
o months later. Neither
s used a great deal and
th were withdrawn in 1977.
M.W.Greenwood

Midland Red introduced a new style touring coach, the C.4, in 1953. Built to the maximum dimensions of 30' 0" by 8' 0", it was fitted with a B.M.M.O.-built 32-seat central entrance body. The bodywork style was generally based on the C.1 and C.2 types, the major difference being the use of curved corner glasses, two flat fixed front windscreens and full-width bumpers. In the following year 63 C.3s were taken into stock. The bodies were built by Willowbrook of Loughborough to the same style as the B.M.M.O. C.4 prototype but seated 37 passengers, being intended for general purpose coach work. Eleven production C.4s were also built in that year with Alexander, the Scottish coachbuilders, producing the 32-seat bodies, again to the same style as the prototype. On 30 August 1966 C.4 4246 (UHA 246) unloads at Digbeth coach station. The outward opening centre entrance door was a notable Midland Red feature that survived into the forward entrance motorway coach era.   A.G.Willis

52

The Flowers Ales must have been a strong temptation to the passengers on Willowbrook-bodied C.3 4181 (UHA 181) at Stratford-upon-Avon bus station during the Summer of 1963. With all central entrance designed coaches the two front seats adjacent to the driver were always very prestigious!

The C.4s were always easily distinguishable from the C.3s by the roof mounted curved glass quarter lights on each side. Whilst engaged on an extended tour, 4251 (UHA 251) takes a well-earned rest at the Lizard Point Cafe during August 1961. All C.4s were upseated to the same capacity as the C.3s in 1959 and the majority had their radiator grilles slightly modified.

A.G.Willis

Seventeen C.3s were selected for rebodying with modern Plaxton 36-seat front entrance coachwork in 1962 and 1963. Designated C.L.3, the rebuilt coaches were nearly two feet longer than originally and replaced the C.4s on extended tours. On a glorious June day in 1963 C.L.3 4190 (UHA 190) passes through Stafford during its first season in rebuilt form. The C.3 Class was withdrawn over the period 1965-7, the C.4s in 1966, and the C.L.3s in 1970-1.

A.G.Willis

In 1954 Midland Red
introduced the prototype
of their very advanced
S.14 Class. Over the
period 1955 to 1959
218 production models
were manufactured in
what was possibly the
most varied of all
B.M.M.O. types. The
S.14 was Midland Red's
first integral
(chassisless) saloon
bus. Every attempt
was made to save
unnecessary weight and
a remarkable unladen
weight of just over
five tons was achieved.
Most of the class had
single rear wheels and
a small number were
fitted with fully
automatic transmission.
S.14s were fitted with
either 40- or 44-seat
bodywork built at
Midland Red's Carlyle
works and which carried
many new innovations,
the most notable being
a new oval design
radiator grille. An
early production S.14,
4257 (UHA 257), is
ready to leave the
temporary bus station,
Lichfield, on
1 May 1961 for
Coventry via the 765
route.   A.G.Willis

The S.14s under
construction entered
service as one-man
operated 40-seaters
but most earlier
examples were later
converted with either
42, 43 or 44
seats. In mid-August
1966, 4697 (697 BHA)
from the final batch,
converted in the
early 1960s, had a
full load of
passengers at
Shrewsbury. A.G.Willis

Many S.14s had variations to the rest of the class. Fitted with an all glass fibre body, 4673 (673 BHA) lasted in this form until withdrawal in 1970. Other S.14 variations included a number fitted with hopper ventilators instead of the normal sliding type, some with twin rear wheels, 4310/47 and 4573 fitted with non-standard engines, 4716 with air suspension and 4671 with exterior advertisements.   B.M.M.O.

The 40-seat dual purpose variant of the S.14 was introduced in 1957 and designated the S.15. Slight modifications were made to the S.14 specification to bring them up to true dual purpose standard. The red and black livery showed the S.15 off to good effect with hopper ventilators, polished aluminium mouldings, deep windscreens and twin rear wheels all being standard. A splendid photograph shows an immaculate S.15 4621 (621 AHA) about to make a right turn into Derby bus station on Sunday 3 September 1961. The driver ignores his trafficator and makes good use of the signalling window. Following 4621 is a 1958 Willowbrook-bodied Leyland Titan P.D.3 belonging to the Trent Motor Traction Company, a keen buyer of pre-war Midland Red products.   P.Kingston

Once conversion to one-man operation had been completed demotion to bus services soon
followed. With this demotion the S.15s regrettably lost their distinctive red and black
livery in favour of the very undistinctive all-over red livery. One of the last S.15s
produced, 5081 (5081 HA), heads down The Parade on a Leamington local service in March 1971.
The S.15s had a relatively short life by Midland Red standards and were withdrawn between
1968 and 1972.   T.W.Moore

S.15s were later converted to one-man operation, and pay-as-you-enter signs were fitted
the front and near side of the vehicles. Plates could be inserted to cover these signs
n the vehicles were being crew-operated and the display was inappropriate. On
uly 1966 Rugby-based S.15 4626 (626 AHA) was at Coventry bus station shortly after
version to O.M.O. and with the above mentioned plates in situ.

econd batch of S.15s was produced in 1962 and these were the last 30' 0" long single-
kers built by B.M.M.O. The second series had additional polished mouldings and the black
ntwork restricted to the roof only. At Stratford bus station, 5075 (5075 HA) contrasted
h S.13 3899 (OHA 899) on 25 May 1963.   A.G.Willis

The C.5 coach was a natural development of the S.14/S.15 models, sharing the basic integral
body framework and mechanical specification. Produced between 1958 and 1961 the bodywork,
built by B.M.M.O., featured a new radiator grille design, a 'lantern'-type windscreen and,
for the first time on a B.M.M.O. coach design, an entrance forward of the front axle. The
C.5 was produced for normal coach duties, however, with the opening of the M1 motorway;
Midland Red introduced Britain's first motorway express coach service, worked by specially
built and now famous C.M.5T Class coaches. (The codes 'M' and 'T' denoted 'motorway' and
'toilet' respectively.) Another variation, the C.M.5, was to the motorway class specification
and similarly fitted with a turbo-charged engine, but lacked the toilet facility. The C.5
and C.M.5 had a capacity for 37, whereas the C.M.5T with the toilet compartment fitted had
capacity for 34 passengers. In 1961 further confusion was caused by the conversion of some
examples of the C.5 Class to type C.S.5. This variation was introduced to increase flexibility
within the class and signified that the vehicle was primarily for use on normal coach duties,
but could be used if required on the high-speed motorway services. On 13 July 1963 C.5
60 4778 (778 GHA) passes through Gloucester Green bus station, Oxford.
P.Kingston

Motorway coach 4808 (808 HHA) was of the toilet-less C.M.5 type and allocated to Nuneaton in August 1960 for use on the Coventry to London motorway service which commenced on 1 September 1960. When photographed on 10 April 1964 it was still allocated to Nuneaton depot and still working the same service. Vehicles regularly employed on the high-speed motorway duties were later fitted with twin headlights. P.Kingston

Brand new C.5 4828 (828 HHA) waits to take its load from Cheltenham coach station to Birmingham in July 1961. Like most of the vehicles in the C.5 classes it was later converted to bus duties (classified C.5A) with an inward opening entrance door. When converted coaches fitted with turbo chargers had their units removed to avoid the possibility of 100m.p.h. service buses!

A number of C.5 coaches found new owners following withdrawal by Midland Red. These included
former 4819 (819 HHA), which was purchased by the Lichfield Speedway Supporters Club in
February 1971. One of the new batch never converted to type C.5A, its distinctive outward
opening entrance door is evident when the vehicle visited Coventry Stadium in September 1978.

T.W.Moore

In 1958 Midland Red unveiled the prototype of a very advanced 30' 0" long high capacity inte
double-decker, the D.9. (The designation L.D.8 had been used for a batch of Leyland double-
deckers in 1952.) It was fitted with a 10.5 litre version of the B.M.M.O. KL engine, which
coupled to an electrically controlled hydraulically operated self-change gearbox and two pec
arrangement. Other advanced features were power steering and variable rate rubber suspensic
with independently sprung front wheels. The 72-seat bodywork was of similar construction to
S.14 with metal framing, aluminium alloy panels and the wide use of glass fibre material.
short fall engine overhang and new low bonnet line afforded improved forward provision from
cab and better accessibility to the engine. Production models first appeared in 1960, of wl
4892 (892 KHA) was representative. 4892 stands beside D.7 4380 (VHA 380) in St.Margarets b
station, Leicester, five and a half years later. The flat windscreen and improved radiator
grille design of the D.9 are of note.

One of the final models furnished with separate moulded mudwings was D.9 5308 (6308 HA) of 1963. Passengers board the Hinckley-based bus at Pool Meadow bus station, Coventry, in May 1966. Leicester, Hinckley and Nuneaton garages all had a share of the working on the frequent 658 service from Leicester to Coventry.   A.G.Willis

21 March 1974 found a dusty D.9 5361 (6361 HA) heading out of Leicester on a very lightly loaded journey on the 650 service to Houghton School. It carries the final Midland Red livery utilising gold fleet names, numbers and legal lettering outlined in black, prior to the implementation of the National Bus Company standard scheme.

M.W.Greenwood

On 1 January 1969 Midland Red became a subsidiary of the National Bus Company set up by the 1968 Transport Act. The N.B.C. at first rationalised the various liveries contained within its fleets and then introduced standard colour shades to its subsidiaries. The first Midland Red bus repainted into N.B.C.'s poppy red livery was early D.9 4851 (851 KHA), which was so treated in August 1972, with a five-inch high hand-painted fleet name, very small fleet numbers and legal lettering. Grey wheel centres complete the vehicle. Later repaints received a white band between decks and one-inch high fleet numbers. The white band considerably improved the appearance of the vehicle, but regrettably was not continued around the front of the D.9 Class. In June 1973 4851 was at the Whitnash terminus outside Leamington Spa.

T.W.Moore

During the mid-1970s the all-over advertisement bus became a very popular way to advertise your business, large or small. Public response varied from outright hostility to happy acceptance. A number of Midland Red D.9s received all-over advertisements, including 5412 (EHA 412D), a 1966 Willowbrook-finished example. It entered service during January 1973 painted into a livery advertising Post Office post codes, utilising poppy red as the basic background colour. In July 1973 it was working Leamington town service L46. Note that the rear destination display of 4851, travelling in the other direction, had been painted over. This policy had been adopted as standard and all vehicles with rear destinations had been similarly treated on repaint.

P.Kingston

The second all-over advertising D.9 treated was 5413 (EHA 413D). This was repainted in July 1972 with a green lower half and white upper to promote the Hall Green Greyhound Stadium, Birmingham. It heads out of the city past the Bull Ring Centre bound for Solihull.

E.V.Trigg

Legal and General Assurance's multicoloured D.9 5422 (EHA 422D), yet another 1966 Willowbrook-finished model, entered service in its new guise in May 1973. It had just left the Bull Ring bus station, Birmingham, when photographed on 30 July 1973. Along with these colourful D.9s further variety was added when most of the ninety vehicles that passed to the West Midlands P.T.E. in 1973 were repainted into the P.T.E.'s blue and cream livery.

M.W.Greenwood

e final 45 models
d their bodies
nished by
llowbrook of
ughborough. On
July 1966 5437
HA 437D) was at
afford, by which
me it was a little
er one month old.
e last D.9, 5445,
so marked the end
B.M.M.O. double-
ck production. The
sign remains unique
d the 345 models
ilt represent one
Midland Red's most
tstanding and
ccessful designs.
    A.G.Willis

A cold wintry morning
in January 1978 found
5357 (6357 HA)
struggling through
the Leicester snows.
Owing to a section of
Scraptoft Lane
becoming impassable
5357 emerges from
Bowhill Grove,
Thurnby Lodge on a
makeshift diversion
route. Incidentally,
an incorrect
destination was being
shown, although the
rigours of the wintry
conditions had made
this facility
superfluous anyway!
Fatigue had, in later
years, caused
difficulty with the
front roof canopies.
The 1964-6 examples
were stiffened with
additional mouldings,
whilst some D.9s,
including 5357, were
subsequently fitted
with plain glass
upper deck front
windows.
    M.W.Greenwood

Withdrawal of Midland Red's D.9s commenced in 1971 with the last examples being delicensed on 31 December 1979. Withdrawn vehicles were often stored, prior to collection by the breakers, in a yard adjacent to Worcester's Padmore Street where cannibalisation could take place. On 7 August 1975 4862 (862 KHA), a former Stratford bus, stands neglected amongst other D.9s, S.16s and lightweight coaches inherited from companies taken over by Midland Red.
P.Kingston

Very few B.M.M.O.-built buses are sold for further use after withdrawal. Most are towed to
the scrapyard, stripped of mechanical units and their remains cut up for scrap. This was the
fate in store for D.9 4999, which was living its final hours at Hudley's scrapyard near
Wednesbury in July 1973. Reports have suggested that 4999 was rescued for restoration to
its former glory by a preservation group. However, considering the extent of work necessary
and the lack of fundamental parts, this seems somewhat unlikely!   M.W.Greenwood

A small number of D.9s did escape the breakers' yard, however, and found further service with other operators. South Wales independent Morris of Pencoed bought a number of D.9s which ran for a time alongside his S.16s and C.M.6Ts! Former 4976 (2976 HA) and 5336 (6336 HA) stand side by side at Morris' yard in Pencoed on 23 September 1975. Painted blue, Morris had the good sense to extend his white band around the front of th vehicles. The mixture of upper deck front windows gives 5336 a 'Nelson' look!

The most fascinating after service sales were seven examples sold to Obsolete Fleet London, who had them converted into open to configuration and then hired them to London Transport for sightseeing tours of London. A photograph on the upper deck of former 4959 reveals th novel retention of the opening ventilators at the front of the vehicle! On this occasion it was about to perform another journey on service 74Z between Baker Street and Regents Park (London Zoo).

M.W.Greenwoo

O.M.7 in the Obsolete Fleet and former 4917 (917 KHA) were being put to good use on the 'Round London Sightseeing Tour' when photographed on 30 June 1975. Four of the original seven D.9s were to be used in 1980, with the possibility of Obsolete Fleet purchasing further examples from Midland Red.

A.B.Cross

Midland Red were impressed by the high capacity front entrance double-deckers being produced by other manufacturers, but not with the unreliable rear engined concept which accompanied their design. The result was the introduction in 1960 of the first D.10 prototype. The new vehicle was fitted with an underfloor engine which represented a revolution in design. Very similar in styling and use of parts as the D.9, the main problem to contend with was the accommodation of the large engine under the floor without raising it, and hence the vehicle height, to an unacceptable dimension. The problem was solved by the Midland Red designers and engineers by placing the engine the opposite way round to that of the single-deckers. The first example, numbered 4943 (943 KHA), was a 78-seat vehicle, whilst the second prototype 4944 (1944 HA), built in 1961, was originally built as a 65-seat version with a second staircase at the rear and a narrow exit door behind the rear axle. The twin staircase experiment was not successful and in 1962 4944 was rebuilt to a single staircase front entrance 77-seater. Early in 1964 both D.10s moved to Stafford, where they spent the rest of their careers, 4944 being seen shortly after its move to Stafford and in rebuilt condition.

A.G.Willis

pproaching Coventry
us station, 4943 when
ew in 1961.
                T.W.Moore

grettably the D.10
sign was not put
to production and
th vehicles had
en withdrawn by
73. The second,
44, ended its life
the scrapyard,
t fortunately 4943
rvived and is now
the careful
nership of the
rmingham and Midland
nibus Trust, perhaps
presenting one of
e most important
hicles within the
S.V. preservation
vement.
                M.W.Greenwood

In 1962 the company introduced a 52-seat version of the S.14 which took advantage of the new legal maximum dimensions of 36' 0" by 8' 2½" wide for coaches and single-deck buses. Designated S.16, the first batch was built in 1962-3. Although numerically the first, 5094 (5094 HA, below) was delivered during 1963 as an additional vehicle. It therefore received a later S.17 smooth body style which compares with normal representative 5123 (5123 HA, opposite). On 5 July 1966 5094 was leaving Nuneaton bus station for Lichfield, whereas 5123 was displaying a later style livery at Leamington in June 1973.

A.G.Willis/T.W.Moore

77

The S.16 was not totally successful, mainly because it was underpowered. In 1963 the company introduced the S.17, a similar vehicle in appearance but fitted with the larger 10.5 litre engine and a semi-automatic two pedal control gearbox. Rather surprisingly, another batch of S.16s entered service in 1964. They were originally intended to be S.17 models but were constructed as S.16s to use up stocks of manual gearboxes and B.M.M.O. 8 litre engines. 5523 (6523 HA) leaves Church Street for Croop Hill on a Rugby local service in March 1971.

T.W.Moore

Withdrawals of the S.16 Class occurred early, in 1973. Examples from both batches were retained to augment the training fleet. Painted into the distinctive all-over yellow liv[e] adopted for the training fleet, S.16 5114 (5114 HA) negotiated Birmingham's Bull Ring on [a] wet day in June 1977.

T.W.Mo[ore]

This photograph of 5517 (6517 HA) clearly depicts the duplicate set of clutch and brake pedals and the location of the instructor's seat.

M.W.Greenwood

The S.17s were constructed over the period 1963 to 1966. Numerous minor changes were made, and from 1964 all new examples were fitted with a D.9 style emergency window to conform with revised statutory regulations introduced at that time for high capacity single-deckers. The majority of S.16s and S.17s were later converted to one-man operation, generally retaining their original seating capacity. A large number of S.17s had only their main body structures completed at Carlyle Road Works, being finished by outside contractors. Willowbrook finished the body of 5605 (BHA 605C), whereas the body of 5765 (EHA 765D) was completed by Plaxton. Both were working Rugby local services in February 1975, by which time they had been converted for one-man operation. Illuminated displays were fitted in the front and near side of 5605, although on this occasion they were not lit! Both vehicles also wear early N.B.C. corporate livery of poppy red with grey wheel centres.

T.W.Moore

Plaxton-finished S.17 5764 (EHA 764D) of 1966 wears the penultimate N.B.C. corporate livery, featuring a white band below the windows. The contrasting architectural designs and the Rugby Clock Tower make an impressive backdrop in this August 1977 view. It was withdrawn from service in the following year. Mechanical experimentation in the S.17 Class was rare: one vehicle, numbered 5093 (5093 HA), although basically an S.17 had a modified form of suspension and became the solitary S.19. (The code S.18 was used on a batch of 1962-3 Leyland single-deckers.) In addition to this vehicle, 5707 ran for a time with a Bristol Siddeley torque converter transmission and 5772 ran with a Leyland 0680 engine between 1971 and 1975.

T.W.Moore

In December 1973 fourteen S.16s and 79 S.17s passed to West Midland P.T.E. together with Midland Red services within the West Midlands metropolitan county. Working on a Stourbridge local service, S.17 5762 (EHA 762D) unloads a number of bemused passengers. It was the first B.M.M.O. bus repainted into the P.T.E.'s blue and cream livery, although it retained B.M.M.O. interior colour scheme. Repainting was done in most cases by Midland Red on behalf of the P.T.E.

T.W.Moore

other livery
riation was applied
1965 Plaxton-
nished S.17
84 (CHA 684C). It
s the first Midland
d single-deck
l-over advertisement
hicle. It
-entered service
ring March 1974 in
mainly blue and
ite livery,
vertising Carrefour
permarket, operating
om Wellington garage.
reverted to normal
livery in April
75 and was withdrawn
years later.

ree vehicles
722-4) were built
1965 as red and
ack liveried, dual
rpose versions of
e S.17 and
signated S.21A
pe. In addition to
e usual S.17 style
iding windows,
723 (DHA 723C) had
rced ventilation
rough the rear
of scoops.
1967 they were
classified S.22
d in 1970 they were
nverted to O.M.O.
t retained their
al purpose status.
June 1971 all
ree were
designated S.17,
th 5723 being
nverted to a
-seat bus in
y 1972 and the
her two being
milarly treated in
cember 1975. On
July 1966 5723
aves Nuneaton for
reford on the
2-mile long X91
rvice which
mmences in
icester.

A.G.Willis

The success of Midlan
Red's high-speed
motorway services
quickly necessitated
the development of
larger and more
powerful machines. Th
result was a prototyp
36' 0" long by 8' 2½"
wide coach which
entered service in
1963 designated C.M.6
The framework was bas
on that used for the
S.17 and in appearanc
it was virtually a
lengthened C.M.5T.
Originally fitted wit
a manual gearbox, thi
was later changed to
the two pedal
semi-automatic type.
Originally this model
was fitted with the C
'lantern' style front
screen but this was
replaced by a four pi
slightly inclined fla
screen with curved
corner glasses. The
seating capacity wher
new was 46, but this
was reduced to 44 wit
general refurbishing.
B.M.M

An imposing late night photograph, taken on 23 December 1977, of S.17 5766 (EHA 766D) at
Coventry's Pool Meadow bus station. It is about to make a return journey to its home town
of Rugby. The S.17 was an extremely competent service bus and probably Midland Red's most
successful single-decker from the lightweight era. The S.16 Class was withdrawn between
1971 and 1976, the S.19 in 1975 and the S.17 between 1975 and 1979.   T.W.Moore

In 1965-6 29 production models were built. Five were 46-seat C.M.6 coaches without toilets for the Birmingham to Worcester motorway services whilst all the others were 44-seat C.M.6T versions. Mechanically they were the same as the prototype but they were very different externally. A six-bay body and new style front and rear end was evolved. In June 1966 5653 (BHA 653C) was on the Coventry bypass bound for Birmingham. The bodywork had an attractive businesslike look about it, ideally suited to its role as a motorway coach.

Between January 1972 and May 1973 eighteen members of the class entered Carlyle Road Works for overhaul and restyling. Bus type destination boxes were affixed in the front dome, and deep polished mouldings were added at waist level. In June 1972 5652 (BHA 652C) became the first Midland Red coach to receive N.B.C. white livery. Initially it retained its silver Midland Red style fleet name and number. It is seen shortly after repaint parked at Warwick Castle coach park whilst working on a private charter.
R.C.Hor

The white livery was not the best choice for a coach continually subjected to demanding motorway work, and it soon looked shabby. These splendid coaches were destined for a relatively short life and they were withdrawn between 1972 and 1974. As with the D.9s a number were stored for some considerable time at the Padmore Street yard, Worcester. A side-on view of withdrawn 5662 shows it in the final N.B.C. coach livery. This particular coach was based at Nuneaton for the Nuneaton-Coventry-London motorway service, and it carr the appropriate details in the side mounted destination displays.
M.W.Greenw

Only three C.M.6Ts avoided the scrapyard after withdrawal. Until sold to a dealer in mid-1975, 5662 and 5663 (DHA 962/3C), withdrawn in April 1974, remained at the Worcester dumping yard. Before passing to Morris of Pencoed, where it joined former stablemate 5662, 5663 had a spell with Turriff, the contractors, and Catterall Coaches of Southam. It retained a yellow and white livery that it had received during its second career, whereas 5662 was painted into Morris' blue and white livery. Both were in Pencoed when photographed on 23 September 1975. The two were soon on the move again, having a spell with Everton's Coaches, Droitwich, before 5663 ended its life in a Bromsgrove scrapyard. Meanwhile, the career of 5662 continues, having been purchased by a private buyer with the intention of converting it into a touring caravan!

M.W.Greenwood

The third vehicle was 5656 (BHA 656C) which, following withdrawal, was purchased by the Midland Red Preservation Society (Leamington) in August 1975. It subsequently passed into the Birmingham and Midland Motor Omnibus Trust collection as a representative of Britain's only coach totally designed and built for high-speed motorway duties.   P.Kingston

The final series of B.M.M.O.-built buses was a variation of established principles. All were 36' 0" long by 8' 2½" wide and mechanically almost identical to the S.17 type. The body structure was based on the six-bay C.M.6 production coaches, coupled with S.17 style front windscreen, emergency window and entrance door. The most notable difference was the fitting of a single piece rear window and the lack of rear destination number box. Thirty 49-seat S.21 semi-coaches entered service in 1967. (The S.20 designation was used for conventional Willowbrook-bodied Leyland semi-coaches.) The side windows were fixed and forced ventilation was incorporated, and they were intended primarily for light weekday stage carriage work and weekend coach duties. Polished aluminium mouldings were used liberally, especially at the front end which was of a new and attractive design. The red and black livery further enhanced these vehicles, although a number were finished in a newly-introduced red and maroon livery. In September 1967 5865 (JHA 864E) was photographed at Coventry's Pool Meadow bus station. From 1970 they were fitted for O.M.O., generally retaining original seating although 49-, 51- and 53-seat versions appeared in small numbers.

T.W.Moore

A Kidderminster S.21 5857 (JHA 857E) has received N.B.C. poppy red bus livery by August 1973 but had retained its original seating.
M.W.Greenwood

-travelled S.21 (LHA 878F) nded bus rallies over the country its Rugby-based f. The staff Rugby garage to preserve vehicle when s finally drawn from ice. It stands de a member of famous London sport RT Class transport ering held at site of the toft trolleybus um in July 1978.
M.W.Greenwood

The S.21s/S.22s had two door luggage compartments provided at the rear end. Later in li
with the demotion to normal bus work, the boots were panelled over. Demotion had occurr
by the time this photograph of 5906 (PHA 506G) at Tamworth on 12 October 1977 was taken.
Although fitted for O.M.O. service 765, 5906 was still crew operated at that time.
                                                                        M.W.Greenw

Immediately following the semi-coach variants 37 45-seat dual purpose buses designated S.22
were built. Fitted from new for one-man operation, their function was to work the longer
distance stage carriage services and private hire work. Overall the S.22 echoed the S.21,
with the most noticeable change being a front end more akin to the S.17 type and a radiator
grille not dissimilar to that of the D.9 double-decker. Displaying an incorrect destination,
5881 (MHA 881F) heads out of Coventry on its way to Nuneaton in December 1976.   T.W.Moore

During the snows of February 1979 S.22 5885 (MHA 885F) makes its way through Thurma
village on a Leicester local service.
                                                                        M.W.Green

The final B.M.M.O. production programme comprised 75 S.23 O.M.O. fitted service buses.
Built between 1968 and 1970 they were very similar to the S.22 Class except that they were
fitted with 51 seats, windows incorporating top sliding ventilators and no luggage boot.
Bus number 5941 was the last complete B.M.M.O.-built vehicle which entered service in
January 1970. The remaining fifty vehicles had bodywork completed by Plaxton's of
Scarborough and the very final S.23, 5991, entered service in June 1970. A 1969 machine,
5932 (RHA 932G), nears Meriden when new.   T.W.Moore

On 22 July 1979 Plaxton-finished S.23 5977 (UHA 977H) was many miles from home, arriving at the London Bus Rally, Brockwell Parking, having just completed the London road run. It is in the final N.B.C. livery of poppy red with white band and roof mounted fleet name. The fleet name in this position allowed a revenue-earning advertisement to be placed under the lower saloon windows. It passes a selection of preserved London Transport RF Class saloons. A small number of S.21s, S.22s and S.23s continued to give faithful service at the start of the 1980s.

►

Soon after the control of the company passed to the National Bus Company, it was announced that vehicle building was to cease. N.B.C. naturally collected the blame for this decision, but for some years vehicle production had been hopelessly uneconomical and N.B.C. or not, there is no doubt that the decision to end vehicle building was inevitable. Preserved S.12 3750 (NHA 750, overleaf) complete with Coronation fittings at the 1978 Showbus Rally reflects the marvellous character of the early post-war B.M.M.O. single-decker.

M.W.Greenwood